The
Cat-Lovers'
Cookbook

The Cat~Lovers' Cookbook

Recipes by Tony Lawson
Illustrations by Paté Lawson

Created and developed by Kingsley Barham
Foreword by Dr. David S. Kronfeld
University of Pennsylvania, School of Veterinary Medicine

A Storey Publishing Book

STOREY COMMUNICATIONS, INC.
POWNAL, VERMONT 05261

Please Note

It is our intention to give you sufficient knowledge and instruction to maintain your cat's health and general well-being. The authors and Storey Communications, though, cannot be responsible for any illness or reaction that may result from the consumption of the recipes, or from employing the cat health care tips, contained herein. If there are any indications or symptoms that give you concern, seek veterinary advice promptly.

Cover and text design by Wanda Harper
Typesetting by Hemmings Motor News,
    Bennington, Vermont, in American Typewriter
Printed in the United States by R.R. Donnelley &
    Sons Company

Third printing, May 1992

Library of Congress Cataloging-in-Publication Data

Lawson, Tony, 1954-
  The cat-lovers' cookbook.

  "A Storey Publishing book."
  1. Cats — Food — Recipes. I. Title.
SF447.6.L39 1986   636.8'085 86-45042
ISBN 0-88266-426-3

Dedication

To Bruce Barham, and his "herd" of Abyssinians, who first recognized the need for a serious nutritional document for cat lovers.

To our precious pets who have provided us with so much love and joy: Pippin, Tito, Haleakala, Gangi, Baby Kitty, Bowleggie, Felton. Annie, MacArthur, Serrano, Olive, Snow, and Tuxedo.

Contents

Foreword

Reciprocation is the basis of our relationship with cats. We have selected their species as companions for our own pleasure, and hopefully they enjoy us in the same way.

Our impositions on their nature have taken away from cats the primitive ability to make choices for their own personal welfare. We now make some, though by no means all, important decisions in their lives. One of the main choices that a cat owner faces is the diet that will be best for his or her pet. This book offers gastronomic pleasures: recipes that work, that are balanced nutritionally, that are palatable for cats, and fun for us to cook.

These recipes represent an alternative to commercial cat food. Proprietary pet foods are a triumph of technology: they are processed to convert the by-products of human food (essentially "nonfood" for humans) into food for pets. By contrast, the inspired recipes of Tony Lawson use real human food as a basis for nutritious and delicious food for cats.

Today's cat remains an obligatory carnivore, locked into its past. The cat's biochemistry and behavior fall into patterns much more narrow than those of its evolutionary cousin, the dog. The cat's avid penchant for animal protein, for instance, reflects the inability of its liver to regulate the break-

down of amino acids. Most animals have this con-
serving ability, but the cat's forebears never needed
it because their diet contained plenty of protein. The
cat also remains attached to specific dietary requirements for vitamins such as retinol and niacin,
and amino acids such as arginine.

The cat does <u>not</u> thrive on diets used to feed dogs.
So if one wishes to cook for cats, one must take care,
exceedingly good and enlightened care, to do it
right. The recipes in this book that are declared fit
to use everyday are sure to promote buoyant health
in kittens and cats. Those not in this category may
be used once or twice a week.

All of these recipes offer opportunities for pleasure and togetherness. As the Romans, who first
domesticated cats to guard their granaries, used to
say:

Symbiotica et sympatico hominum
philapussicat est.*

Dr. David S. Kronfeld
Clark Professor of Nutrition
School of Veterinary Medicine
University of Pennsylvania

*Symbiotic and sympathetic is the person who loves
pussycats.

Acknowledgments

We want to thank Dr. David S. Kronfeld for his patience, his insights, and his enthusiasm. The vast amount of research material that he provided to us proved invaluable toward our goal of creating a nutritionally credible cookbook for cats.

We are grateful to Drs. L. D. Lewis and Mark L. Morris for permission to reprint their special diet recipes. They appear as Appendix Table 3, "Recipes for Homemade Dietary Foods," in Small Animal Clinical Nutrition, published in 1984 by Mark Morris Associates, Topeka, Kansas 66606.

We especially want to thank the friends and relatives of Tony and Paté Lawson and Kingsley Barham who offered their interest and excitement, help when it was needed, and peace and quiet when we had to have it.

And thank you to the Lord of Creation, who created everything, especially cats.

The
Cat-Lovers'
Cookbook

¶Introduction

Whether you are trying out one of these recipes to reward your cat for catching that pesky mouse or because it just sounds like something new and fun to do, the purpose of this book is to offer you a fun collection of nutritional treats for your feline pal.

It is also our intent to provide you with enough knowledge of your pet's dietary needs so that you can whip up any variety of nutritionally sound homemade treats on your own. Pay particular attention to the four supplements mentioned in Dr. Kronfeld's "Theme Recipe." They are: liver, corn oil, bone meal, and iodized salt. These supplements are what provide a majority of the vitamins, minerals, and fatty acids that are essential in a cat's diet. Also look at the assortment of Kitty Tips throughout the book. They will provide you with additional information on nutrition, food preparation, ingredient substitutions, and other practical tips on caring for your cat.

We have included a section in the book entitled "Tandem" recipes. These are simple recipes for people, but with only slight modifications they can be suitable for your cat as well. Care should be taken to provide the correct proportions of protein, carbohydrates, and the supplements in your cat's diet, as described by Dr. Kronfeld's "Theme Recipe."

Most of the recipes herein provide anywhere from

1 to 6 servings. Be sure to label and date leftover portions. They can be safely refrigerated for <u>only</u> 3 to 4 days, or frozen. Do not feed anything to your cat that has been in the refrigerator longer than 4 days, or which smells at all suspect.

Our primary goal is to help you enjoy (and maintain) a healthy, happy cat. We hope you enjoy the recipes and the special humor on the pages that follow.

The
Kronfeld Diet
for Cats

Many cat fanciers have asked the author of our Foreword, Dr. David S. Kronfeld, how to cook for their cats. His "Theme Recipe" uses ground meat and rice as staples because they are main sources of energy. The supplements to this theme recipe are designed for convenience and to provide all of the essential nutrients not found in the staples: liver, bone meal, corn oil, and iodized salt.

The Theme Recipe

2/3 cup ground meat
1/3 cup dry rice (brown or white)
2 tablespoons chopped liver
1 tablespoon bone meal
2 teaspoons corn oil
1/2 teaspoon iodized salt
1 cup water

Bring the water to a boil. Add the rice, corn oil, and salt, and simmer for 20 minutes on low heat. Dredge the meat with the bone meal. Add the meat and liver to the rice mixture, stir, and simmer for another 15 minutes.

Cool and serve. Yields 3 servings. Leftovers should be refrigerated or frozen.

Variations on the Theme Recipe

The meat used in the theme recipe is usually hamburger with a medium fat content. Fat cats may benefit from lean meat or an organ meat such as heart. Meat may be replaced by fish. Some types of fish are fatty (salmon, for example), and others are lean (such as flounder). Cats also love chicken, turkey, goose, and duck — all of which may replace meat.

Rice can be replaced by barley, potato, canned or frozen corn, or tapioca. But rice is hard to beat for cats because it is easily digested and blends well with other foods.

Liver is needed every day, or nearly every day, to provide necessary trace minerals and vitamins. It may be replaced by other organ meats, such as kidney or sweetbreads, but none have the potency and benefits of liver.

One way to handle liver, and have it easily available, is to freeze it as "liver ice cubes." Chop a pound of liver into quarter-inch cubes. Divide the pile into sixteen equal portions. Put one portion into each of the sixteen compartments of an ice cube tray. Each portion equals one ounce. Freeze the liver in the tray, and pop out "liver ice cubes" as needed.

Another easy way to prepare liver for your cat's consumption is to cook it, and then roll it between two sheets of cellophane so that it resembles a thin pancake. You can then freeze it in the cellophane and break off the amount you want as needed.

The easiest way to cook liver is to chop it into very small (kitty-bite-size) pieces and then boil it for about 15 minutes. Be sure to drain it well.

4

Steamed bone meal is available at many health food and pet stores, and is a good source of calcium. It can be replaced by other good sources of calcium such as milk and dairy foods, or green leaf vegetables. As part of your cat's diet, calcium is not necessary every day, but we suggest that you make it available two or three times a week.

Corn oil provides vitamin E as well as essential fatty acids. It may be replaced by wheat germ oil fortified with vitamin E.

It is easy to modify the theme recipe to accommodate cats that are susceptible to F.U.S (feline urological syndrome). Prepare the recipe as you would normally. Instead of adding ½ teaspoon iodized salt, add 1 full teaspoon iodized salt, and instead of using 1 tablespoon bone meal, use 1 teaspoon calcium carbonate. (Crushed TUMS tablets or finely ground eggshell are good sources of calcium carbonate.)

A teaspoon or two of chicken fat added to a cat's food will tempt even finicky felines and build up scrawny kitties.

If your cat is on a weight loss diet, you will find tripe an economical alternative to meat, and it has the added advantage of being virtually fat-free.

Wheat bran may be substituted for rice in a feline weight reduction diet. When using wheat bran, double the amount of water required to cook rice. Wheat bran has the benefit of not only being lower in calories, but its high fiber content fills the digestive tract and gives a sense of fullness.

Calcium is less efficiently absorbed by cats when they are on a cereal diet. Soybeans, in particular, compound this problem because they contain an organic compound, phytin, which binds calcium to itself and further inhibits absorption.

Vegetable greens are high in calcium and can be chopped and added to most feline recipes. Try beet greens, swiss chard, collards, dandelion greens, kale, mustard greens, parsley, spinach, and turnip greens.

There are five readily available calcium supplements:

- meat and bone meal

- bone meal (steamed)

- dicalcium phosphate

- calcium carbonate

- ground limestone

Meat and bone meal and steamed bone meal are considered the most palatable; limestone the least palatable.

Fin

Kitty
Jambalaya

⅓ cup ground beef
1 clove garlic, finely chopped
¼ cup onion, diced
¼ cup tomato, diced
⅔ cup rice, uncooked
⅓ cup chicken, cut into kitty-bite-size pieces
⅓ cup shrimp, cut into kitty-bite-size pieces
⅓ cup fish, <u>boned</u> and cut into kitty-bite-size
    pieces
2 cups water
2 teaspoons corn oil
2 teaspoons bone meal
2 tablespoons liver*
1 teaspoon iodized salt

    Fry ground beef in medium saucepan. Remove meat from pan. Add garlic to pan and simmer briefly. Add onion, tomato, and rice; stir fry until onion is clear and soft. Add the rest of the ingredients and stir. Cover and simmer for 15 minutes. Stir mixture to blend ingredients and simmer for 10 more minutes. Let cool, then serve. Yields 5 to 6 servings.
    Store unused portions, in an airtight container and keep refrigerated.
    This recipe is fit for everyday use.

*Please refer to page 4 for instructions on how to prepare liver for use in this and all subsequent recipes.

You Gotta Have Sole

½ pound fillet of sole
2 tablespoons onion, chopped
2 tablespoons parsley, chopped
salt and pepper
water
1 tablespoon butter
1 tablespoon flour
½ cup milk
¼ cup cheddar cheese, grated
2 tablespoons liver
½ teaspoon iodized salt
⅔ cup cooked noodles, cut into kitty-bite-size
   pieces (or cooked rice)

Put sole in a small, greased baking dish. Sprinkle with onion, parsley, and a dash of salt and pepper. Add enough water to just cover the bottom of the dish. Cook in a preheated 450° oven for 10 minutes. Remove from oven, cool, and cut into kitty-bite-size pieces.

Melt butter in small saucepan. Stir in flour and heat until bubbling. Gradually stir in milk and cook, stirring constantly until mixture thickens. Add cheese, liver, and salt; stir until cheese has melted. DO NOT BOIL. Add chopped fish and noodles to cheese sauce and stir well. Cool and serve. Yields 4 to 6 servings.

Store unused portions in an airtight container and keep refrigerated.

This recipe is fit for everyday use.

Tuna
Cakes

2 eggs
1 6½-ounce can tuna, drained and flaked
1 small onion, finely chopped
4 slices bread, cubed into kitty-bite-size pieces
½ teaspoon iodized salt
1 teaspoon brewers yeast
1 teaspoon bone meal
2 tablespoons margarine

Beat eggs lightly in bowl. Add tuna, onion, bread cubes, salt, brewers yeast, and bone meal. Mix thoroughly until moistened. Form into small patties. Melt margarine in skillet and fry patties until golden brown. When cool, crumble each patty and serve. Yields 3 to 5 servings.

Store unused portions in an airtight container and keep refrigerated.

Fish with a high quantity of fat include salmon, tuna, mackerel, herring, and white fish. The fat in these fish is rich in vitamins A and D and is a good source of protein for cats. If your cat is on a weight reduction diet, lean fish would be a better choice.

Sardines
and Rice
(Kitty Heaven)

2 flat cans of sardines in oil
2/3 cup cooked rice
1 tablespoon liver
1/4 cup parsley, chopped

Combine all ingredients in mixing bowl. Use a wooden spoon to stir and break up sardines into kitty-bite-size pieces. Serve immediately. Yields 2 to 3 servings.

Store unused portions in an airtight container and keep refrigerated.

Kitchen wastes, bones, and rotten food can injure or cause serious illness to your cat; therefore, be sure your garbage cans have secure lids that will prevent access by your pet.

Fish
Chowder

½ pound fish, <u>boned</u> and cut into kitty-bite-size
    pieces
1 cup creamed corn
¼ cup potato, chopped fine
2 tablespoons onion, chopped fine
1 clove garlic, minced
1 tablespoon margarine
1 cup milk
1 tablespoon liver, chopped
½ teaspoon iodized salt
grated cheese (optional)

Combine all ingredients in medium saucepan.
Cover and simmer for 20 minutes. Cool and serve
plain or topped with grated cheese. Yields 4 to 5
servings.

Store unused portions in an airtight container
and keep refrigerated.

This recipe is fit for everyday use.

Bones can cause chok-
ing or even damage to a
cat's digestive tract.
Properly dispose of fish,
chicken, and other
bones, and take care to
keep your cat away from
these hazardous dinner
scraps.

15

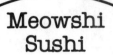

Meowshi Sushi

⅓ cup rice, uncooked
⅔ cup chicken broth
1 teaspoon corn oil
⅓ cup carrot, grated
1 6½-ounce can tuna, drained and flaked
½ teaspoon brewers yeast

Cook rice in broth with corn oil. After about 15 minutes, but <u>before</u> all the liquid is absorbed, add grated carrot. When the liquid is absorbed, set aside. Cool, mix in flaked tuna, and serve. Sprinkle with brewers yeast. Yields 2 to 3 servings.

Store unused portions in an airtight container and keep refrigerated.

Boogaloo
Shrimp

½ cup onion, chopped
1 tablespoon margarine
¼ pound shrimp, cooked and shelled
¼ cup sour cream
½ teaspoon iodized salt
1 teaspoon brewers yeast
⅔ cup rice, cooked

Finely chop onion and sauté in margarine until light brown. Add shrimp to onions and stir until heated through. Remove from heat and stir in sour cream, salt, and brewers yeast. When cool, mix with the cooked rice, and serve. Yields 2 to 3 servings.

Store unused portions in an airtight container and keep refrigerated.

A fish-only diet is definitely unbalanced. Not only is it deficient in some minerals, but can also cause a loss of vitamin E. If you take care to include the basic nutritional supplements (liver, bone meal, corn oil, iodized salt) in fish recipes, this condition can be corrected.

Cod, haddock, flounder,
and bass are lean fish.
They should be used for
cats on weight reduction
diets because they are
far leaner than the lean-
est meat. Lean fish
should not constitute
more than 70 percent of
a cat's total diet, in order
to allow for the addition
of essential vitamins
and nutrients from
other food sources.

Fish is rich in flourine, iodine, and zinc.
Some fish contain an enzyme that reduces
the ability to absorb thiamine, a vitamin
which is essential to normal metabolism
and nerve function. This enzyme, thiamin-
ase, is destroyed by the cooking process.
Therefore, it is a good idea to cook all fish
prior to serving.

Feather

Chicken
With Greens

⅔ cup chicken with giblets (especially the liver)
1 cup tomato juice, or ½ cup tomato puree and ½
    cup water
⅓ cup rice, uncooked
½ cup turnip or beet greens, chopped fine
1 clove garlic, minced
½ teaspoon iodized salt
1 teaspoon corn oil

Cut chicken and giblets into kitty-bite-size pieces.
Bring tomato juice to a low boil in a covered saucepan. Add chicken and rice, cover, and simmer for 15
minutes. Add greens, garlic, and salt. Cover and
simmer for another 10 minutes. Remove from heat
and stir in corn oil. Cool before serving. Yields 2 to
3 servings.
    Store unused portions in an airtight container
and keep refrigerated.
    This recipe is fit for everyday use.

Chicken
Chow Mein

2 tablespoons corn oil
¼ cup green pepper, chopped fine
¼ cup red pepper, chopped fine
¼ cup onion, chopped fine
1 tablespoon flour
2 teaspoons bone meal
½ cup chicken broth
1 tablespoon soy sauce
½ teaspoon iodized salt
dash of pepper
¼ cup mushrooms, chopped fine
½ pound chicken breast, cooked, and cut into
   kitty-bite-size pieces
2 tablespoons liver
1½ cup cooked egg noodles, cut into kitty-bite-size
   pieces

Heat corn oil in saucepan. Add green pepper, red
pepper, and onion; sauté until onion is soft and
translucent. Sprinkle with flour and bone meal.
Gradually stir in chicken broth, cover, and simmer
for 10 minutes. Add soy sauce, iodized salt, dash of
pepper, mushrooms, chicken, and liver. Simmer
another 10 minutes. Remove from heat and stir in
noodles. Serve cool. Yields 4 to 6 servings.
   Store unused portions in an airtight container
and keep refrigerated.
   This recipe is fit for everyday use.

Chicken
Salad

1 tablespoon corn oil
1 tablespoon celery, chopped fine
1 tablespoon onion, chopped fine
1 tablespoon bell pepper, chopped fine
⅓ cup chicken, cooked and cut into kitty-bite-size
   pieces
2 tablespoons ricotta cheese
2 tablespoons plain yogurt or sour cream
½ teaspoon iodized salt
1 teaspoon brewers yeast
¼ cup alfalfa sprouts, chopped

Heat oil in skillet. Add celery, onion, and bell
pepper to skillet and cook until soft. Let vegetables
cool. In mixing bowl combine the rest of the ingredients, except for the alfalfa sprouts, and mix well.
Stir in cooled vegetables and chopped alfalfa sprouts
and serve. Yields 2 to 3 servings.
   Store unused portions in an airtight container
and keep refrigerated.

who said
that cats are
boring pets?

Hair Balls

A hair ball is an accumulation of hair in a cat's stomach as a result or his or her own grooming. This can occur even if you brush your pet regularly. Symptoms are a dry cough, vomiting after meals, and/or constipation. You can help your cat eliminate hair balls by applying a bit of petroleum jelly to the end of his or her nose to lick off.

Combing is the best way to prevent hair balls. Long-haired cats need a combing two or three times a week, but for short-haired cats once a week is fine.

The natural shedding season for cats is during the spring, and to a lesser degree, the fall. Cats may also shed because of stress (illness, moving, owners away on vacation) or because of dry indoor heat used during the winter months. During the shedding season, try to schedule a few extra grooming sessions.

Gizzard
Goulash

1 tablespoon corn oil
½ pound chicken gizzards and/or hearts chopped
    into kitty-bite-size pieces
¼ cup onion, chopped fine
1 clove garlic, minced
½ teaspoon paprika
½ teaspoon iodized salt
1 medium tomato, chopped fine
1 tablespoon liver, chopped
1 cup cooked macaroni noodles (or other noodles
    chopped into kitty-bite-size pieces)
¼ cup sour cream

Heat oil in skillet. Add chicken gizzards and
lightly brown. Add onions and garlic to skillet and
sauté until onion is tender but not brown. Blend in
paprika and salt. Add tomato and liver, cook about 3
to 5 minutes, stirring constantly until tomato has
become soft and runny. Remove from heat, stir in
the noodles and sour cream. Cool and serve. Yields 3
to 5 servings.

Store unused portions in an airtight container
and keep refrigerated.

This recipe is fit for everyday use.

Chicken
Soup

½ cup lentils

2 cups water

2 chicken breasts, boned and cut into kitty-bite-
size pieces

¼ cup carrot, chopped fine

¼ cup broccoli, chopped fine

1 clove garlic, minced

⅓ cup onion, chopped fine

1 teaspoon iodized salt

2 teaspoons bone meal

2 tablespoons corn oil

2 tablespoons liver (cooked or raw)

Place lentils in 2-quart pan, add water, and bring to a boil. Lower heat, cover, and simmer for 30 minutes. Add remaining ingredients to pan and simmer another 15 to 20 minutes, stirring occasionally. Cool and serve by itself or over dry food. (If your cat is known to pick out his or her favorite flavors, you can try putting a portion in the blender on a low setting for just a few seconds to create a finer consistency.) Yields 4 to 5 servings.

Store unused portions in an airtight container and keep refrigerated.

This recipe is fit for everyday use.

Heaven... I'm in Heaven

Chicken
and Asparagus
Casserole

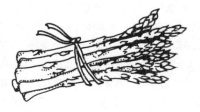

²/₃ cup cooked chicken, boned and cut into kitty-
    bite-size pieces
²/₃ cup cooked elbow macaroni (small size)
1 stalk asparagus, chopped fine
1 tablespoon chopped liver
2 tablespoons milk
2 tablespoons ricotta or cottage cheese
1 teaspoon corn oil
½ teaspoon iodized salt
2 tablespoons cheddar or white cheese, grated

Combine oil ingredients except grated cheese in
medium size mixing bowl and stir to blend. Put mixture in small, well-greased casserole or small glass
bread pan and top with grated cheese Bake in preheated 375° oven for 20 minutes. Cool and serve.
Yields 3 to 4 servings.
    Store unused portions in an airtight container
and keep refrigerated.
    This recipe is fit for everyday use.

If yours is an indoor cat, it may help to prevent hair balls to keep a little pot of grass available. Keep the grass pot in a place that your cat frequents: by a sliding glass door or on a favorite window sill. Just make it accessible to your cat for occasional nibbling.

Grass and other vegetable matter is fibrous and is not easily digested by cats. These fibrous materials tend to absorb water, expand, and soften, which provides bulk in the digestive tract. This helps to carry hair and other nonorganic residues out in the feces.

Turkey
Surprise

1 ½ cups water
1 teaspoon iodized salt
2 teaspoons corn oil
½ cup rice, uncooked
½ pound turkey giblets,
    chopped into kitty-
    bite-size pieces
¼ cup carrot, chopped fine
½ cup chopped spinach

Add salt and oil to water and bring to a boil. Pour
rice in boiling water, lower heat, cover and cook for
10 minutes. Stir in turkey giblets, carrot, and spinach. Cover and simmer on low heat for another 10
or 15 minutes. Cool and serve. Yields 4 to 5
servings.

Store unused portions in an airtight container
and keep refrigerated.

This recipe is fit for everyday use.

Hoof

"Hearty"
Beef

½ pound beef heart, cooked and chopped
1 tablespoon corn oil
1 clove garlic, minced
¼ cup spinach, chopped fine
¼ cup onion, chopped fine
2 eggs
¼ cup corn meal
½ teaspoon iodized salt
2 tablespoons chopped liver

To prepare beef heart, simmer in water for 15 to 20 minutes. Let cool and chop into kitty-bite-size pieces.

Heat corn oil in skillet. Add garlic and sauté briefly (30 seconds). Add spinach and onion and sauté until onion is soft and translucent. Beat eggs in medium mixing bowl. Blend corn meal and salt with eggs. Mix in beef and liver. Add mixture to skillet and stir well; continue to cook until eggs are done. Cool and serve. Yields 3 to 4 servings.

Store unused portions in an airtight container and keep refrigerated.

This recipe is fit for everyday use.

You may add one teaspoon of salt to any of the recipes in this book to help promote water intake.

33

Lamb Stew

1 tablespoon corn oil
½ pound boneless lamb, cut into kitty-bite-size pieces
3 tablespoons flour with a dash of salt
1 clove garlic, minced
1½ cups water
½ teaspoon iodized salt
1 pinch basil
1 small carrot, minced
¼ cup onion, minced
¼ cup peas, frozen or fresh (slightly mashed if needed)
½ cup corn, slightly chopped if larger than bite size
½ cup potato, cut into kitty-bite-size pieces
2 teaspoons bone meal
¼ cup liver

Heat oil in medium saucepan. Dredge lamb in flour and add to skillet. Lightly brown lamb on all sides. Add garlic to lamb and sauté another minute. Add water, salt, and basil. Cover and simmer 15 minutes. Add carrot, onion, peas, corn, potato, bone meal, and liver. Cover and simmer approximately 15 minutes until potatoes and carrots are done. Cool and serve. Yields 4 to 6 servings.

Store unused portions in an airtight container and keep refrigerated.

This recipe is fit for everyday use.

Kidney
Stew

1½ cups water
1 tablespoon corn oil
1 teaspoon iodized salt
½ pound beef kidney, cut into kitty-bite-size pieces
½ cup rice, uncooked
1 carrot, chopped fine
4 mushrooms, chopped fine
2 tablespoons tomato paste
1 teaspoon bone meal

Place corn oil and salt in water and bring to a coil. Put kidney, rice, carrot, mushrooms, and tomato paste into boiling water. Cover and simmer on low heat for 20 minutes. Remove from heat and stir in bone meal. Cool and serve. Yields 4 to 6 servings.

Store unused portions in an airtight container and keep refrigerated.

This recipe is fit for everyday use.

It's okay by me!

Tisk-Tisk-Tisk — I think she forgot something in this one!

Beef or Pork
With Bean Sprouts

½ pound ground beef or pork
1 tablespoon soy sauce
1 clove garlic, minced
1 tablespoon corn oil
¼ cup green beans, cut into kitty-bite-size pieces
¼ cup mushrooms, chopped fine
½ cup bean sprouts, chopped fine
1 teaspoon corn starch
¼ cup chicken broth
½ teaspoon iodized salt
½ to 1 cup cooked rice
2 tablespoons liver, chopped
2 teaspoons bone meal

Mix meat with soy sauce and garlic, and marinate for 20 minutes or longer. Heat oil in skillet. Add meat mixture and lightly brown. Add green beans and sauté about 2 minutes. Add mushrooms and sauté another 2 minutes. Add bean sprouts and sauté 2 more minutes. Mix corn starch with chicken broth in a bowl, add to skillet and heat until sauce has thickened; stir in iodized salt. Remove from heat and stir in rice, chopped liver, and bone meal. Cool and serve. Yields 4 to 6 servings.

Store unused portions in an airtight container and keep refrigerated.

This recipe is fit for everyday use.

Muscle meat is deficient in calcium, copper, iodine, vitamin A, and riboflavin. Cereal grains are deficient in calcium, riboflavin, niacin, protein, and fat. The combination of liver, bone meal, iodized salt, and corn oil as a dietary supplement will act to correct these deficiencies.

Killer!

Meat is rich in iron and phosphorus. Unlike the iron in vegetables, the iron and phosphorus in meat is more efficiently absorbed into your cat's system.

Both meat and cereal contain very little calcium. It is advisable, therefore, to add calcium supplements (dicalcium phosphate, steamed meat and bone meal, and steamed bone meal — all available in pet stores) to recipes that feature meat or cereal. Be careful to add only the amounts recommended on the supplement's package because too much calcium can diminish the absorption of other nutrients.

Kitty-Size
Lasagna

½ pound ground beef
pinch of oregano
¼ clove garlic, minced
¼ teaspoon iodized salt
1 lasagna noodle, cooked (approximately ⅓ cup)
½ cup tomato paste
1 teaspoon olive oil
¼ cup cottage cheese or ricotta cheese
1 teaspoon brewers yeast
2 tablespoons cheddar cheese, grated

Add oregano, garlic, and salt to beef and lightly brown in skillet. Cut cooked lasagna noodle into kitty-bite-size pieces. Add noodles, tomato paste, and olive oil to skillet and heat through. Remove from heat, and mix in cottage cheese and brewers yeast. Top with grated cheddar cheese. Serve when cool. Yields 3 to 4 servings.

Store unused portions in an airtight container and keep refrigerated.

Substituting liver for brewers yeast, and corn oil for olive oil, will make this recipe fit for everyday use.

Kitty
Pizza

½ pound ground beef
1 teaspoon corn oil
1 clove garlic, minced
2 tablespoons onion, chopped fine
2 tablespoons bell pepper, chopped fine
1 tablespoon olives, chopped fine
1 tablespoon mushrooms, chopped fine
½ teaspoon oregano
1 teaspoon iodized salt
½ cup tomato puree (or ¼ cup tomato paste and
   ¼ cup water)
2 tablespoons liver
¼ cup mozzarella cheese, grated
½ cup French bread, cut into kitty-bite-size pieces
2 tablespoons Parmesan cheese, grated

Heat oil in skillet. Add ground beef and lightly brown. Add garlic and sauté 1 minute. Add onion and bell pepper and sauté until both are soft. Add olives and mushrooms and sauté 2 minutes. Sprinkle with oregano and salt. Add tomato puree and liver and simmer 2 to 3 minutes. Turn heat to low and stir in mozzarella cheese. Remove from heat when melted. Stir in French bread and let cool. Serve topped with Parmesan cheese. Yields 4 to 6 servings.

Store unused portions in an airtight container and keep refrigerated.

This recipe is fit for everyday use.

Feline mother's milk has three times the protein of cow's milk, but much less milk sugar and fat. This is why some cats can't tolerate cow's milk, though most cats can become accustomed to it if they are introduced to it gradually.

Kittens need about twice the calories per body weight as an adult cat in order to meet the nutritional demands of their growing bodies. It is a good idea to have food available for kittens at all times and allow them to feed freely.

Growing kittens require between two and four times the amount of quality protein in their diets than most mammals. About 30 percent of the available energy in their diet should come from good quality protein: meat, fish, eggs, and dairy products.

Pregnant and nursing cats have special needs. They will experience an increase in appetite because they have a greater need for protein, vitamins, and minerals. Make sure that they always have fresh water available, and allow them plenty of sleep. Add a midday meal to their feeding schedule, and you may want to add a vitamin supplement to their diet as well.

Beef and Bean Sauté

1 tablespoon corn oil
1 clove garlic, minced
½ pound ground beef
⅓ cup green beans, chopped fine
½ teaspoon iodized salt
⅓ cup cooked rice
1 tablespoon liver
½ teaspoon bone meal

Heat corn oil in skillet. Add garlic and sauté quickly (approximately 30 seconds). Add ground beef and cook until lightly browned. Add chopped green beans, stir, and continue cooking until beans are soft. Add salt, rice, liver, and bone meal, and toss until well mixed. Let cool and serve. Yields 4 to 6 servings.

Store unused portions in an airtight container and keep refrigerated.

This recipe is fit for everyday use.

The starch in cereals tends to inhibit how efficiently food energy, protein, calcium, iron, zinc, and copper are assimilated. Therefore, recipes that are high in cereal content need to have liver, bone meal, iodized salt, and corn oil added to give your cat a well-rounded meal.

Kitty
Taco

½ pound ground beef
½ cup onion, chopped fine
2 tablespoons bell pepper, chopped fine
1 clove garlic, minced
1 tablespoon tomato paste
1 teaspoon corn oil
1 corn tortilla, cut into kitty-bite-size pieces
½ teaspoon bone meal
½ teaspoon brewers yeast
½ teaspoon iodized salt
2 tablespoons cheddar cheese, grated

Heat skillet and start browning ground beef.
When meat is half cooked add onion, bell pepper,
and garlic, and cook the mixture until onions are
translucent and the meat golden brown. On low
heat, stir in tomato paste, corn oil, chopped tortilla,
bone meal, brewers yeast, and salt. Stir until heated
through. Cool and serve topped with grated cheese.
Yields 2 to 3 servings.

Store unused portions in an airtight container
and keep refrigerated.

Mixing one teaspoon
of mineral oil with your
cat's food once or twice a
week will help prevent
hair balls and
constipation.

Kitty
Bath

1 kitty
1 kitchen/utility sink or plastic basin
1 towel or rubber mat
3 to 4 inches of warm water
1 ounce of cat shampoo, or tearless shampoo for
  humans
1 plastic cup
2 dry, warm towels
1 grooming brush or comb

Optional: creme rinse
             hair dryer
             mood music

Remove loose hair with a gentle combing or
brushing. Prepare sink or basin with 3 to 4 inches
of warm water and place a towel or rubber mat on
the bottom to keep your cat from slipping. Add one
cat to the water. Using a large rubber cup, douse his
or her head with warm water, then the rest of the
body. Run shampoo down the full length of the cat.
As you work the shampoo into a lather from head
to tail, be very careful not to get soap in your cat's

eyes or ears. To make long fur easier to comb after the bath, you may want to finish with a little creme rinse.

Your cat will need a final rinse of warm, clean water to ensure that all shampoo residue is removed from the skin, which should prevent drying and irritation. Wrap your cat in a warm towel and dry carefully. A second towel can be used to dry your pet thoroughly; gently rub the towel against his or her skin. A hair dryer on the warm setting can be used to finish drying and fluffing — if your cat is still cooperating, and hasn't decided the whole idea is for the birds.

Other:
Eggs and Cheese

Western Scramble for Kitty Roundups

1 tablespoon margarine
¼ cup chopped ham or cooked ground beef
2 tablespoons chopped bell pepper
2 tablespoons chopped tomato
2 eggs
¼ teaspoon iodized salt
1 tablespoon milk or plain yogurt
2 tablespoons cheddar cheese, grated
3 teaspoons sour cream
1 teaspoon brewers yeast

Heat margarine in skillet. Add meat, bell pepper, and tomato. Sauté until bell pepper is soft. Beat eggs, salt, milk or yogurt, and add to the meat mixture. Add the cheese and scramble on low heat until firm. Top each portion with 1 teaspoon sour cream and a pinch of brewers yeast. Yields 2 to 3 servings.

Store unused portions in an airtight container and keep refrigerated.

Raw egg whites contain a protein called avidin that impairs the absorption of vitamin B. Cooking eggs will inactivate avidin, making them more nutritious and easier to digest.

It is not advisable to add raw eggs to your pet's diet because they have been known to cause salmonella poisoning in animals. We recommend that you either cook eggs or pour boiling water over eggs in their shells before you feed them to your pet — this should kill any salmonella bacteria. The avidin in the egg will be inactivated by this process, and should help with the digestion and absorption of vitamin B.

Cheese Scramble

3 eggs
3 tablespoons cheddar cheese, grated
2 tablespoons milk or plain yogurt
2 tablespoons alfalfa sprouts
1 teaspoon brewers yeast
½ teaspoon iodized salt
1 tablespoon margarine

Mix all ingredients except margarine in a medium mixing bowl. Heat margarine in skillet until melted and add the egg mixture. Scramble on low heat until the eggs are cooked. Cool and serve. Yields 2 to 3 servings.

Store unused portions in an airtight container and keep refrigerated.

Kitty on the Run
(A quick and easy recipe)

⅓ cup cottage cheese
2 tablespoons Bisquick
1 tablespoon chopped liver
1 tablespoon corn oil
dash of iodized salt

Mix all ingredients thoroughly and serve. Yields 1 to 2 servings.

Store unused portions in an airtight container and keep refrigerated.

This recipe is fit for everyday use.

51

Brewers yeast is a great source of high-quality protein and vitamins. It has been used as a substitute for liver in some of the recipes, but because it lacks vitamin A, vitamin C, and some trace minerals, it should be used as a liver substitute only occasionally.

Corn oil is not only a good source of fatty acids essential to a healthy diet for your pet, but is also a good source of vitamin E.

Cheddar cheese is a good source of fat and protein, and is rich in vitamin A and riboflavin. It may be substituted for meat in most recipes, or grated and sprinkled on top of food to tempt the finicky eater.

Kitty
Fondue

1 teaspoon corn oil
1 clove garlic, minced
1 cup cheddar cheese, grated
½ cup condensed cream of chicken soup
½ teaspoon iodized salt
¼ cup chicken broth
2 tablespoons liver
1 cup French bread, cubed to kitty-bite-size pieces

Heat oil in saucepan. Add garlic and sauté 1 minute. Add cheese, soup, and salt. Stir constantly over low heat until cheese has melted and mixture is creamy. Remove from heat and stir in chicken broth and liver. When mixture has cooled to lukewarm stir in French bread and serve. Yields 3 to 4 servings.

Store unused portions in an airtight container and keep refrigerated.

This recipe is fit for everyday use.

If your pet has common diarrhea, you may treat it with Kaopectate. Using an eye dropper, administer one teaspoon toward the back of your cat's mouth, as often as five times a day when symptoms occur. If the diarrhea persists after one day, call your veterinarian.

Your cat may run a fever for many reasons, and there are any number of possible symptoms. Some of these are listlessness, lack of appetite, vomiting, or diarrhea. You can use a rectal thermometer to check the temperature of your pet if you suspect that he or she is running a fever. A cat's normal temperature is between 100.5°F and 102°F. If your cat's temperature is higher than 102°, call your veterinarian.

An antiseptic ointment that is suitable for small children is a convenient way to treat minor cuts and scrapes on your cat.

Tandem Cooking

Beef
Stroganoff

For People

8 tablespoons butter
2 medium onions, sliced fine
16 mushrooms, sliced fine
2 pounds beef tenderloin, cut into strips
1½ cups sour cream
salt and pepper to taste

Cut beef into ½-inch by 2-inch strips. Melt 2 tablespoons of the butter in a skillet. Sauté onions until golden brown and remove from skillet. Add 1 tablespoon butter to skillet and sauté mushrooms for about 5 minutes. Remove mushrooms from skillet. Heat remaining butter in skillet until it is bubbling and then add half of the beef. Quickly brown all sides of the meat for about 5 minutes. Remove the cooked beef and brown the remaining beef. Put all beef, onions, and mushrooms back into the skillet and stir to heat through. Add salt and pepper to taste and continue to stir while adding the sour cream. Heat until it nearly boils. Serve immediately over rice. Yields 6 people servings; or 4 to 5 people servings and 1 portion for your cat.

For Kitty

⅔ cup Beef Stroganoff
⅓ cup cooked rice
1 teaspoon brewers yeast

Chop Stroganoff into kitty-bite-size pieces. Combine Stroganoff, rice, and brewers yeast, and stir well. Serve cool. Yields 2 to 3 servings.
Store unused portions in an airtight container and keep refrigerated.

Shish
Kebab

For People

2 to 2½ pounds lamb, boneless shoulder, boneless
rib, or loin chops

Vegetable suggestions (choose any or all):
mushroom caps
bell pepper, cut into squares
tomato, quartered (or cherry tomatoes)
pearl onions
zucchini, 1-inch-thick slices, halved
garlic cloves

Fruit suggestions (choose any or all):
pineapple chunks, fresh or canned (canned will
provide juice for marinade)
lime or orange chunks
banana, thick slices
cantaloupe or honeydew melon chunks
apple chunks
spiced crab apples, whole

Cut lamb into 1- or 1½-inch cubes. Place in bowl
or deep dish and pour enough marinade to cover
meat. Lift and separate pieces so that all sides of the
meat are coated with marinade. Let stand in refrigerator at least 2 hours, but preferably overnight.

After it has marinated, combine the meat, vegetables, and fruit on skewers. Be creative with combi-
nations. Place skewers on hot barbecue or under
broiler. Turn and baste with reserved marinade as
necessary until the lamb is done to your taste and
kebab is browned evenly. Keep an eye on the kebabs
while cooking because they can burn quickly. Yields
6 people servings; or 4 to 5 people servings and 2 to
3 kitty servings.

Marinade

1½ cups soy sauce
1 cup wine vinegar
1 cup pineapple juice
¾ cup brown sugar
1 teaspoon salt
2 cloves garlic, minced

Combine ingredients in mixing bowl and stir well. Reserve left over marinade to use as a basting sauce. Yields about 4 cups.

Kitty Kebab

4 lamb cubes from the shish kebab chopped into kitty-bite-size pieces or ground
¼ cup kebab vegetables, chopped fine
⅓ cup white rice, cooked
1 teaspoon corn oil
½ teaspoon iodized salt
1 teaspoon bone meal
2 tablespoons liver
2 tablespoons marinade

Combine all ingredients in mixing bowl and stir until well blended. Serve cool. Yields 2 to 3 servings.
Store unused portions in an airtight container and keep refrigerated.
This recipe is fit for everyday use.

Chicken
Paprika

For People

- 1 tablespoon corn oil
- 1 medium onion, chopped fine
- 2 tablespoons paprika
- 1 clove garlic, minced
- 1 teaspoon iodized salt
- 1 cup water
- 1 3-pound chicken, skinned, boned, and cut into bite-size pieces
- 1 green onion, chopped
- 1 carrot, chopped fine
- 2 medium potatoes, cut into small cubes
- ½ cup chicken broth
- 2 tomatoes, chopped
- 1 red bell pepper, chopped fine
- 1 green bell pepper, chopped fine
- parsley

In a 4-quart saucepan, heat oil, and sauté the onion. Sprinkle 1 tablespoon paprika over onion and stir well. Add garlic, salt, and ½ cup <u>hot</u> water. Cover and simmer over low heat for 10 minutes. Add chicken and rest of water, then simmer another 20 minutes. Add green onions, carrot, potato, and chicken broth. Simmer for 10 minutes. Add tomato, red and green bell pepper, and 1 tablespoon paprika. Stir all ingredients together and simmer 10 more minutes. Garnish with fresh parsley and serve. Yields 6 people servings; or 4 to 5 people servings and 1 portion for your cat.

For Kitty

1 cup Chicken Paprika
¼ cup cooked rice
½ teaspoon brewers yeast
½ teaspoon bone meal

Chop Chicken Paprika by hand or use blender to obtain small enough pieces for your cat. Mix rice, brewers yeast, and bone meal with Chicken Paprika. Serve cool. Yields 2 to 3 servings.

Store unused portions in an airtight container and keep refrigerated.

Both onion and garlic have a reputation for warding off fleas. Whether or not this is the case, our animals seem to love the taste of both. A little sautéed minced onion and/or garlic, a little pressed fresh garlic, or even a pinch of garlic powder, will entice your cat to eat a new or unpopular dish.

How to Make a Kitty Gift Bag

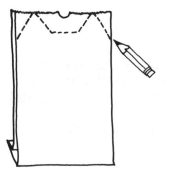

1. Using a flat-bottomed bag you get at the grocery store, trace ears on the front side of the bag and cut them out.

2. Be creative and draw your favorite cat friend on the front side of the bag with a colored marker.

3. Place gift item, wrapped in tissue paper, inside the bag.

4. Staple closed at the three spots indicated by arrows.

When transporting kitty to the vet or kennel, don't run the risk of losing your pet in an unfamiliar area or on a busy street. Purchase a cardboard cat carrier at a pet store before taking your cat in for his or her first visit to the veterinarian or kennel.

Salmon
Loaf

For People

 1 12-ounce can salmon, skinned, boned, and
   drained
 ½ cup evaporated skimmed milk
 2 slices white bread, cut into small cubes
 2 eggs, slightly beaten
 ¼ cup celery, chopped fine
 ¼ cup green onion, chopped fine
 ½ teaspoon dill
 1 teaspoon lemon juice
 ¼ teaspoon thyme
 dash of salt and pepper
 1 tablespoon melted butter

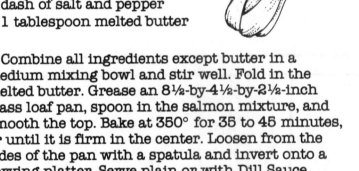

Combine all ingredients except butter in a
medium mixing bowl and stir well. Fold in the
melted butter. Grease an 8½-by-4½-by-2½-inch
glass loaf pan, spoon in the salmon mixture, and
smooth the top. Bake at 350° for 35 to 45 minutes,
or until it is firm in the center. Loosen from the
sides of the pan with a spatula and invert onto a
serving platter. Serve plain or with Dill Sauce.
Yields 4 people servings; or 3 people servings and 1
or 2 servings for your cat.

Dill Sauce

⅔ cup cucumber, peeled, seeded, and chopped fine
1 cup sour cream or plain yogurt
2 tablespoons sugar
1 tablespoon white wine vinegar
1 tablespoon Dijon mustard
1 tablespoon dill weed
½ teaspoon salt

Combine all ingredients and refrigerate for 30 minutes before serving.

For Kitty

⅔ cup Salmon Loaf
½ teaspoon bone meal, or one-half of the bones removed from the canned salmon, <u>if</u> they are soft
½ teaspoon brewers yeast

After the Salmon Loaf has cooled, break up ⅔ of a cup into a bowl. Mix in either the bone meal or the salmon bones (if soft) and the brewers yeast. Yields 1 to 2 servings.

Store unused portions in an airtight container and keep refrigerated.

Water should be available to your cat at all times. Some cats prefer fresh water and others prefer to have the same dish topped off each day. Whatever your cat prefers is best — a healthy allowance of water everyday will help to prevent problems.

It is a good idea to "cat proof" your house. Damage can result to both pet and property unless precautions are taken.

- If kitty likes to perch on the window ledge, be sure that the windows and screens are secure.
- Keep small toys, objects, and potted plants picked up and well out of reach. An adventurous cat may try to eat anything that is small enough or easily accessible.
- Electrical cords to lamps, televisions, and appliances should be concealed as much as possible. Your cat may try to play with any loose cord and end up pulling down a lamp or appliance.
- If cats are allowed to pull or chew on electrical cords they may seriously burn, or even electrocute, themselves. Unplug all cords to nonessential or unused electrical appliances, and don't leave them dangling. This is especially important if you are leaving your pet alone in the house for a few days.

One of the simple joys in life is so inexpensive.

Rabbit Stew

For People

2 2½- to 3-pound rabbits, boned and cut into bite-size pieces
½ cup flour
½ pound bacon, sliced
½ cup onion, chopped fine
2 cloves garlic, minced
½ cup red wine
1½ cups chicken broth
2 tablespoons sherry (optional)
⅛ teaspoon rosemary
⅛ teaspoon thyme
salt and pepper to taste

Season rabbit pieces with salt and pepper and dredge in flour. Fry bacon until crisp; drain, crumble, and reserve drippings. Heat bacon drippings in a large pan or skillet and brown rabbit pieces. Set aside. Drain all but 2 tablespoons of the bacon drippings, and brown onion in pan. Add garlic and cook 1 minute. Add wine and chicken broth and bring to a boil, stirring constantly to deglaze the pan. Stir in the rest of the ingredients including the crumbled bacon. Add rabbit pieces, cover and simmer for 1 hour. Yields 6 people servings; or 4 to 5 people servings and 1 portion for your cat.

For Kitty

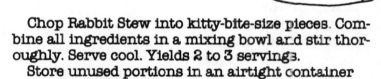

> 1 cup Rabbit Stew (mostly meat)
> ½ cup cooked rice
> 1 tablespoon cooked liver
> ½ teaspoon bone meal
> ½ teaspoon iodized salt
> 1 teaspoon corn oil

Chop Rabbit Stew into kitty-bite-size pieces. Combine all ingredients in a mixing bowl and stir thoroughly. Serve cool. Yields 2 to 3 servings.

Store unused portions in an airtight container and keep refrigerated.

This recipe is fit for everyday use.

Chicken
Cordon Bleu

For People

5 tablespoons chopped ham
5 tablespoons grated Swiss cheese
1 clove garlic, minced
1 tablespoon white wine
5 boneless chicken breast halves (1 for your cat)
$\frac{1}{3}$ cup flour
$\frac{1}{2}$ teaspoon iodized salt
dash of white pepper
1 large egg
1 teaspoon corn oil
$\frac{1}{3}$ cup dried bread crumbs
4 tablespoons butter
$\frac{1}{4}$ cup corn oil for cooking

Mix ham, cheese, and garlic with the white wine. Divide the ham and cheese mixture into 5 equal portions. Place 4 chicken breasts skin side down and spread a portion of ham and cheese mixture over each breast. Roll each breast up and tie closed with string or secure with toothpicks. Refrigerate for 20 to 30 minutes.

Combine flour, salt, and white pepper, and dredge each chicken breast with flour mixture.

Beat egg with 1 teaspoon corn oil and carefully brush each breast with egg mixture. Roll each breast in bread crumbs. Heat $\frac{1}{4}$ cup corn oil and butter in skillet and fry chicken breasts until golden brown and cooked through (10 to 15 minutes per side on medium/low heat). Drain and serve. Yields 4 people servings.

For Kitty

- 1 tablespoon butter
- 1 chicken breast (with skin), chopped into kitty-bite-size pieces
- 1 portion ham and cheese mixture
- 1/3 cup cooked rice
- 1/2 teaspoon bone meal
- 1/2 teaspoon brewers yeast

Heat butter in skillet. Lightly brown chopped chicken. On low heat, stir in ham and cheese mixture and rice. Stir until heated through. Remove from heat and stir in bone meal and brewers yeast. Serve cool. Yields 2 to 3 servings.

Store unused portions in an airtight container and keep refrigerated.

When checking the label of commercial cat food, look for a statement of nutritional adequacy: that the product is complete and balanced for the nutritional maintenance of an adult cat.

Hill's Diets for Cats With Special Dietary Needs

The following recipes are for cats with special dietary needs. These recipes are the work of a well-known veterinary nutritionist, Mark L. Morris Jr., D.V.M., Ph.D. Dr. Morris co-authored, with Dr. Lon D. Lewis, the textbook entitled, Small Animal Clinical Nutrition. This textbook is recognized worldwide as an authoritative source on small animal nutrition, has been translated into Japanese and French, and is used in schools of veterinary medicine throughout the world.

These recipes are so specialized that they are not recommended for cats that are, in general, healthy. If you suspect that your cat has a problem that would require a special diet, we recommend that you consult your veterinarian before starting your pet on one of these dietary programs.

Questions about these recipes, or the commercially produced prescription diets, can be addressed directly to the manufacturer: Hill's Pet Products, Department of Consumer Affairs, P.O. Box 148, Topeka, Kansas 66601. Their toll-free number is, (800) 255-0449.

The Why of Special Diets

We all know people on special diets. The heart patient may be avoiding foods high in sodium; the overweight teenager counts calories; and the expectant mother makes sure her diet is nutritious and well-balanced.

Cats and dogs have health problems similar to people and, like people, need to follow a modified diet that is different from that of the average pet.

Your veterinarian may recommend a special diet for your pet if there are indications that it will be necessary. Perhaps your cat has a food-related allergy or an intestinal disability. Maybe she's stubbornly overweight, or she could have a chronic kidney or liver disorder. Your cat may even be troubled with urinary stoppages. A special diet can help considerably. The following pages explain how the various diets are planned, and how they can help.

Every pet deserves to see a veterinarian at least once a year to check immunities and evaluate overall physical condition. When your pet has a condition requiring a special diet, regular visits to the vet are even more important. Even though your pet appears to be in good health, be sure you do your part to help him or her have a happy, long life.

How to Switch Your Cat to a New Food

It would probably be most effective to abruptly switch your cat to a new food or diet. However, the new food may be quiet different in digestive properties than the old food, so start with a smaller portion than the amount recommended for your cat. Gradually increase the quantity up to the amount recommended to give your cat time to get accustomed to the new food. Too often, a cat is allowed to eat whenever the mood hits, and as a result is never truly hungry. Be patient — appetite will catch up with him or her.

For Food-Related Allergies

If your veterinarian suspects that a food allergy is causing problems for your cat, such as hives (which you may have mistaken for fleas) or diarrhea, he or she may recommend a shift to d/d.

A nutritionally balanced food, d/d is made with hypoallergenic ingredients. If your cat's symptoms are relieved after a period of time on this diet, your veterinarian will know that his or her ailment is related to a food allergy. The veterinarian will suggest the next step. In some cases, the simplest and most humane course is to feed d/d as the exclusive diet for the remainder of your cat's life.

Hill's
Allergy Diet (d/d)

This recipe constitutes a balanced, vitamin-mineral supplement that should be served in a quantity sufficient to provide the daily requirement for each vitamin and trace mineral.

¼ pound diced lamb
1 cup white rice, cooked
1 teaspoon corn oil
1½ teaspoons dicalcium phosphate

Trim fat from lamb. Cook thoroughly (braise or roast) without seasoning. Add remaining ingredients and mix well. Keep covered in refrigerator. Yields ¾ pound.

Feeding Guide for Cats on an Allergy Diet

Feed your cat an amount sufficient to maintain normal body weight.

Body Weight	Approximate Daily Feeding
5 pounds	¼ pound
7 to 8 pounds	⅓ pound
10 pounds	⅖ pound

If it is suspected that the allergy is food related, maintain your cat on the above diet and distilled water. Then expose the patient to various foods, one at a time, to discover the offending products. Begin with tap water, and watch your animal closely for any aggravating symptoms. The aim of this provocative exposure to all kinds of foods is to determine what your cat <u>can</u> eat, rather than what he or she cannot eat.

For a Delicate Intestine

Intestinal upsets stem from a variety of causes. Sometimes a cat ingests highly irritating material, or may have an intestinal infection. A few cats have an unusually sensitive intestinal tract, just as humans may have chronic colitis. In these situations, a bland, nonirritating, and easily digested diet is necessary.

A nutritious, highly digestible food, i/d is made from ingredients unlikely to irritate the intestines. It is often used for cats recovering from abdominal surgery. It can also be used to aid in recovery from diarrhea that is sometimes accompanied by a loss of appetite. Because it is so easily digested and soft, i/d may be prescribed for kittens until their digestive tracts are fully developed. As a diet, i/d places minimum stress on your cat's digestive organs and supplies the nutrients needed for growth, as well as healing and tissue repair.

Hill's Soft
Bland Diet (i/d)

½ cup Cream of Wheat, cooked to make about 2 cups

1½ cups creamed cottage cheese

1 large hard-cooked egg

2 tablespoons brewers yeast

3 tablespoons granulated sugar

1 tablespoon corn oil

1 tablespoon potassium chloride

2 teaspoons dicalcium phosphate

Cook Cream of Wheat according to package directions. Cool. Add remaining ingredients, balanced vitamin-mineral supplement purchased from your vet or pet store, and mix well. Keep covered in refrigerator. Yields 2 pounds.

Feeding Guide

Feed your cat an amount sufficient to maintain normal body weight.

Body Weight	Approximate Daily Feeding
5 pounds	¼ pound
7 to 8 pounds	⅓ pound
10 pounds	⅖ pound

For Obesity

Excessive weight can make your cat uncomfortable. It can also shorten his or her life. The overweight cat may have difficulty exercising or even breathing. Bone structure may be sorely strained and arthritis can result when a cat is carrying extra pounds. Fat may hinder the proper functioning of the heart, liver, or digestive tract.

Reducing your cat's ration of regular food is not the best solution because when you reduce amounts enough to cut calories, you also reduce essential proteins, vitamins, and minerals necessary for good health.

The feline reducing diet (r/d) is low in calories because carbohydrates and fats are reduced to the minimum amount necessary for good health and good digestion. But the r/d does provide an ample supply of protein, vitamins, and minerals. This diet is suitable for cats with a history of F.U.S. (feline urological syndrome) because mineral levels are restricted.

Hill's
Reducing Diet
(r/d)

This recipe constitutes a balanced, vitamin-mineral supplement that should be served in a quantity sufficient to provide the daily requirements for each vitamin and trace mineral.

1½ pounds pork liver, cooked and ground
1 cup cooked rice
1 teaspoon cooking oil
1 teaspoon calcium carbonate

Combine all ingredients. Yields 1¾ pounds.

Feeding Guide

Body Weight	Approximate Daily Feeding
5 pounds	¼ pound
7 to 8 pounds	⅓ pound
10 pounds	½ pound

Snacking and scavenging should be absolutely forbidden during the reducing period. After the cat attains an ideal weight, a quality maintenance diet at a level which just maintains that weight can be initiated.

For Impaired Liver and Kidney Function

Cats, like dogs and other creatures, can suffer from kidney disorders. The normal kidney helps the body eliminate wastes from food proteins. If the proteins are of excellent quality, the kidneys don't need to work as hard to process the waste products generated by food proteins. Too much protein in a diet can strain diseased kidneys. Therefore, the amount of protein in a cat's diet should be reduced if he or she is suffering from weakened kidneys. Whatever protein a cat does eat should be of a higher quality.

The feline kidney diet (k/d) is a superior nutritional food made with specially selected and carefully balanced proteins. It may be fed to a cat over a long period of time. No other food should be offered to a cat with ailing or diseased kidneys — serious illness could result.

Hill's Feline Kidney Diet (k/d)

This recipe constitutes a balanced, vitamin-mineral supplement that should be served in a quantity sufficient to provide the daily requirements for each vitamin and trace mineral.

> 1 tablespoon fat (bacon grease or cooking oil)
> ¼ pound cooked liver
> 1 large egg, hard-cooked
> 2 cups cooked white rice
> 1 teaspoon calcium carbonate

Brown the liver in the fat. Do not drain fat. Dice or grind liver and egg. Combine all ingredients and mix well. This mixture is somewhat dry, but the palatability may be improved by adding some water (not milk). Yields 1¼ pounds.

Feeding Guide

Feed your cat an amount sufficient to maintain normal body weight.

Body Weight	Approximate Daily Feeding
5 pounds	¼ pound
7 to 8 pounds	⅓ pound
10 pounds	⅖ pound

For Urinary Stoppages

The bodies of some cats cannot manage mineral matter properly. (On ordinary pet food labels, mineral matter may be referred to as "ash.") Mineral crystals in the bladder or urethra gather together to form larger units called calculi, gravel, or stones. The presence of this matter can cause pain during urination, blood in the urine, and even retention of urine (which can cause blood poisoning).

The feline c/d diet is different from any ordinary cat food because the mineral content is only the amount necessary for proper nutrition. Hence, there is less mineral matter available in your cat's system to encourage stone formation. In addition, it is high in protein, fat, vitamin A, and B-complex vitamins, and is easily digested for use by the body.

Hill's Diet For Urinary Stoppages, Restricted Mineral Diet (c/d)

1 pound ground beef, cooked
¼ pound pork liver, cooked
1 cup cooked white rice
1 teaspoon corn oil
1 teaspoon calcium carbonate

Combine all ingredients. Yields 1¾ pounds.

Feeding Guide

Feed your cat an amount sufficient to maintain normal body weight.

Body Weight	Approximate Daily Feeding
5 pounds	⅛ pound
7 to 8 pounds	¼ pound
10 pounds	⅓ pound

Appendix

Emergency Information

Pet's Name _____

Birthdate _____

Breed _____ Sex M / F Neutered _____

Color/Markings _____
   (Keep a good full body picture handy)

Registration Tag # _____

Veterinarian _____

Address _____

Phone # _____

EMERGENCY CLINIC ADDRESS _____

Phone # _____

Vaccination Schedule:

Rabies   _____ _____ _____

Feline Distemper   _____ _____ _____

PARVO   _____ _____ _____

Upper Respira-
   tory Diseases   _____ _____ _____

Other   _____ _____ _____

Known Allergies (to drugs or foods) _____

_____

Other Conditions _____

_____

Emergency Information

Pet's Name _____

Birthdate _____

Breed _____   Sex M / F   Neutered _____

Color/Markings _____
   (Keep a good full body picture handy)

Registration Tag # _____

Veterinarian _____

Address _____

Phone # _____

EMERGENCY CLINIC ADDRESS _____

Phone # _____

Vaccination Schedule:

Rabies   _____   _____   _____

Feline Distemper   _____   _____   _____

PARVO   _____   _____   _____

Upper Respira-
   tory Diseases   _____   _____   _____

Other   _____   _____   _____

Known Allergies (to drugs or foods) _____

_____

Other Conditions _____

_____

Emergency Information

Pet's Name _____

Birthdate _____

Breed _____   Sex M / F   Neutered _____

Color/Markings _____
  (Keep a good full body picture handy)

Registration Tag # _____

Veterinarian _____

Address _____

Phone # _____

EMERGENCY CLINIC ADDRESS _____

Phone # _____

Vaccination Schedule:

Rabies   _____ _____ _____

Feline Distemper   _____ _____ _____

PARVO   _____ _____ _____

Upper Respira-
  tory Diseases   _____ _____ _____

Other   _____ _____ _____

Known Allergies (to drugs or foods) _____
_____

Other Conditions _____
_____

Notes

Notes

Notes

Notes